ALPINE GARDENING
A beginner's guide

By W. F. W. HARDING

THE ALPINE GARDEN SOCIETY

First Published in 1981
Reprinted 1987

© The Alpine Garden Society
Lye End Link, St. John's,
Woking, Surrey, GU21 1SW

Editor: J. E. G. Good, Ph.D.
Artwork: D. B. Lowe

ISBN 0 900048 38 7

Printed by L. Baker (Printers) Ltd.
71 Lombard Street, Birmingham B12 0QU

CONTENTS

Cover: A mature rock garden

Photo: E. N. Woodward

INTRODUCTION

This guide is intended for the real beginner. It aims to dispel any nervousness he may feel about the mystique of alpine gardening and to set him off to a sound start which may serve as a springboard for further progress as experience and enthusiasm grow.

Publications on alpine gardening tend to be divided into those which emphasise that rocks are quite unnecessary for the successful culture of alpine plants and those which frighten the reader by showing him how to build elaborate rock formations, which his common sense tells him must involve the acquisition of many tons of stone, almost certainly at great expense, as well as necessitating major physical effort in the handling of these large stones.

Which way is the beginner to turn? It is important for him to realise that nearly all alpine plants *can* be grown perfectly successfully without the use of rocks, more particularly in "Raised Beds", and the Society is shortly producing a Guide devoted solely to this approach, so I shall only mention it in general outline at the appropriate place. It is, however, still probable that the majority of beginners who aspire to grow alpine plants in their gardens and who, in many cases, have admired them growing in the wild, would like to use their plants in a miniature landscape setting with some rocks to act as foils to their alpine charm.

It is now generally realised that the construction of rock gardens on the grand scale (see p. 17) is, for almost everyone, a thing of the past: but we can, drawing on our knowledge that alpine plants are not dependent on rock for their successful growth, produce a modified form of rock gardening, which still preserves the essentials of the landscaping approach but which only requires the use of relatively modest quantities of stone (see p. 18). In this connection it is interesting to look at photographs of some successful rock gardens to see how, with the years, the plants have spread, and how much less prominent the original rocks have become. And yet if no rocks were to be seen, a far less interesting effect would be produced.

If we were Japanese gardeners the main emphasis would be on the rocks and the plants would play a subservient part. Our national genius in gardening has, however, reversed these roles. The plants are the main actors with the rocks used sparingly to give points of visual emphasis and contrast. It was in acknowledgement of this philosophy that the Society when debating its title at its inception decided, against some opposition, to call itself the Alpine Garden Society rather than the Rock Garden Society. In this it showed a remarkable degree of perception and now, more than fifty years later, the original decision has a particular relevance to the problems we face.

It is essential that the beginner, before he starts out, should have a clear picture in his mind's eye of how he is going to grow his alpines and what will be involved. It is hoped that the information contained in this Guide will enable him to start in such a manner that he will have no subsequent cause to regret initial errors and will, over the years, obtain ever increasing pleasure from his chosen hobby.

THE CHOICE OF SITE

The first question to be decided by the would-be alpine gardener is where his alpine garden should be sited. He may have inherited one of those pitiful rockeries, constructed from odds and ends of completely unsuitable materials, stuck in some corner judged to be unsuitable for the growing of supposedly more demanding plants. He must completely disregard any such unwelcome inheritance and start his planning from scratch.

The principal requirements to be taken into account in deciding the positioning of the alpine garden are:
1. An open aspect.
2. Freedom from tree roots.
3. Freedom from perennial weeds.
4. Satisfactory drainage.
5. Satisfactory integration into the garden design.
6. Possibilities for future extension.

The beginner may feel somewhat daunted at having to consider all these points, especially as he may already have decided that there is only one place where it can go. It is, however, to guard against starting off with such a pre-conceived notion that careful consideration must be given to these six requirements, even if it has to lead to some modification in the layout of the garden. If such an analytical approach is made it will gradually be realised that there are more possibilities than were previously supposed. A wise decision now will avoid many future recriminations.

During this initial planning stage all the possibilities should be quietly mulled over and then, as useful ideas finally begin to crystallise, the proposed alpine garden should be sketched out on paper, preferably to scale. When, after much rubbing out and re-drawing, a plan emerges which promises to be satisfactory, it should be tried out on the ground with the help of pegs, string being stretched round them to give a visual representation of the desired shapes of mounds and valleys. The third dimension of elevation has, of course, to be supplied by the imagination. These shapes can then be adjusted until the eye is satisfied viewing from all angles. This approach is equally valid even if the alpine garden is only going to be a few square yards in extent. Careful thought and planning at this stage always pay off in the long run. There is no point in rushing the planning phase when it can be so much fun and is so important.

An open aspect

Most alpines grow in nature where they get plenty of sunshine. It is true that some species thrive best on north facing rocks where they escape the full intensity of the sun's rays but in our latitudes

2

and elevations it is best to provide an open situation for the benefit of the majority of species and, in the building, contrive some positions where the small minority of shade lovers can be accommodated. Trees, as well as casting shade, present problems of drip and leaf fall and the problems increase rather than diminish with the passage of the years. If, in a small garden, it is impossible to avoid shade from neighbouring trees completely one will have to choose the area shaded for the least number of hours and take care to select shade lovers or shade tolerators for the shadier positions. Having said this I would still emphasise that the choice of as open a site as possible is the most important consideration in siting the alpine garden.

Freedom from tree roots

Tree roots can be a great nuisance even when the trees, due to their positioning, do not cut off the sunlight to any appreciable extent or even overhang the site. Remember that narrow columnar trees still have spreading roots! Tree roots are robbers of both nourishment and water and find the prepared soil of the alpine garden very much to their taste. Even if cut back in the process of construction, they will sooner or later re-occupy their former territory.

Freedom from perennial weeds

In all forms of gardening, competition from perennial weeds is to be avoided, particularly from such obstinately persistent species as Greater and Lesser Bindweed, Ground Elder, Couch Grass and others, capable of spreading by underground roots or rhizomes. In alpine gardening it is even more vital that they should not be present. Therefore if at all possible a site should be chosen from which they are absent. If this is impossible, decisive steps must be taken before construction to eradicate them completely.

The simplest method of eliminating such weeds is to remove every piece of root manually when cultivating the soil. This is more easily done on light than on heavier soils. If it is suspected that, in spite of one's best endeavours, the site has not been cleared completely of the weed in question it will be necessary to fallow it for a period, during which the pieces that have been missed can make fresh aboveground growth. This secondary growth can then either again be removed manually or be sprayed with a systemic weedkiller currently manufactured and recommended against the weed in question. This will affect the whole system of the plant below as well as above ground and will kill it off. It must be emphasised that planting after the use of herbicide must obey the instructions given with the product. With very poor and neglected ground an initial spraying of herbicide should be given a month or so before the start of any cultivation.

When it comes to choosing plants it should be borne in mind that there are one or two so-called "rock plants" which you may be given or sold which can prove almost as difficult to get rid of as the weeds that have been cleared. Foremost amongst these are Snow-in-

3

Summer (*Cerastium tomentosum*) and Thread Rooted Veronica (*Veronica filiformis*).

Satisfactory drainage

Almost all alpine plants dislike bad drainage. Many revel in their native habitats in a plentiful supply of moisture at the roots, largely from melting snow, but this is water on the move which passes on and down and does not exclude air from the soil. Such conditions are impossible to copy in the garden, where the principal aim should be to ensure that the soil cannot become waterlogged.

In the past very sharp drainage has been advocated, involving the provision of a soil composed largely of stone chippings, providing so-called "scree" conditions, but for the beginner, and for most others, such extreme drainage is likely to cause more problems than it solves. Plants will suffer in hot dry weather if not watered and after a few years will exhaust the available nourishment resulting in some portion of the alpine garden always being in a state of renewal.

The aim should be to suit the requirements of the majority of the plants to be grown by providing a happy mean in respect of drainage. This is best achieved by cultivating the area to two full spades' depth if possible and improving the soil's permeability by the generous incorporation of, on the one hand, sharp sand, chippings, boiler ash or any other gritty or opening material, and, on the other hand, horticultural peat or leaf mould which, strangely enough, helps to create a good porous soil whilst at the same time always retaining a reserve of moisture for the plant roots. Naturally the quantities necessary will vary with the initial nature of the soil while rainfall should also be considered, more drainage material being added in wetter parts of the country. A handful of the resultant mixture in a moistened condition should, after being released from compression in the hand, break up easily. Further details on soil preparation are given in the section on construction.

One would hope that the provision of an artificial drainage system would never be necessary, bearing in mind that in the making of an alpine garden the contouring of the ground provides the opportunity to vary the levels between elevated and better drained areas, and lower areas into which water can drain and where a small pool and/or bog garden can, if desired, be located.

Integration into the garden design

Satisfactory integration into the overall design must depend on the exercise of good taste. It has to be conceded that, unless the garden as a whole is carved out of a hillside, the alpine garden can rarely be made to appear as a completely natural feature. Fortunately our eyes and imaginations have become attuned over the years to certain conventions and they are willing to go along with many aspects of our inevitably artificial approach providing that their credulity is not strained too far.

It should be the aim to exploit slopes and changes of level wherever they exist to produce the effect of rock outcropping naturally from the ground. Alternatively, if the garden is more formal and sufficient stone is available to build retaining walls, the slope can be terraced, the crevices of the retaining walls being planted up with an attractive variety of alpine plants. The level terraced areas, with their good drainage, will also grow good alpines. Most gardeners, lacking a sufficient supply of stone for the construction of retaining walls, will opt for gentle contouring of the slope to provide an informal setting for their plants. This use of sloping ground to make an alpine garden has the merit that it capitalises on a change of level whereas, with lawn and many other forms of treatment, such a change is usually a disadvantage. An inherited grassed bank so often represents an undesirable maintenance commitment. The lowering of its gradient by removal of soil from the top to the toe of the bank will enable it to be planted up with alpine plants, with a bare minimum of stone-work protruding at strategic points. Its outline can be varied with some pleasant curves if it is desired to make the effect more informal.

In the only too common case of the garden being completely flat there is no need to despair of making an alpine garden. Some very charming and satisfying creations have been made on just such sites. Whilst on level areas there is the alternative of growing one's alpines in raised beds, as will be explained later in this Guide, if one is really intent on having an alpine garden in the accepted sense of the word it is necessary to set about creating one's own hills and valleys. In this case it is very useful, though not essential, to incorporate a small pool and/or bog garden in the plan. This enables soil to be excavated from the area of the pool and used to create elevated areas.

Grass makes a very good foreground to an alpine garden, bearing in mind that a close-cropped alpine turf often forms an integral part of the mountain scene. For the background it is suggested that the planting should become progressively more shrubby, with shade loving plants such as hellebores, hostas and ferns being incorporated amongst the shrubs. The latter could finally pass into trees if space allows.

These remarks perhaps suggest an alpine garden of some extent but, however small the garden may be, the same principle applies of merging the alpine planting into the neighbouring planting so that the transition is not too sudden and unnatural. In constricted areas it may be necessary for the background to be provided by a wall or a hedge, both of which can be satisfactory, though in the latter case account must be taken of the hedge roots when arranging the planting.

Possibilities for future extension

Artistically it is clearly preferable to plan the whole alpine garden at one time and as one entity and then to carry it out in stages as time and means permit. The beginner is not, however, usually in a position to be so ambitious and far-sighted and in any case, with experience, his ideas will change and develop. He will initially want to try his hand at making a small alpine garden. Experience shows, however, that he is likely to make rapid advances once he becomes really enthusiastic so that, on however limited a scale his initial approach may have been, there is a strong probability that, as he gains in expertise and is wanting to grow an ever increasing range of plants, he will find his first alpine garden too small for his needs. He should therefore envisage this possibility from the outset and locate it where there is room for further extension.

CONSTRUCTION AND PLANTING

Once the important decision has been taken on the positioning of the alpine garden and a plan has been produced showing the general layout and extent, the next stage is that of turning this conception into a reality. Different approaches will be considered to suit the amount of stone available. The construction and planting will be dealt with under the following headings:
1. Preparing the ground.
2. Selecting the stone.
3. Contouring the ground and fixing the rocks.
4. Making and stocking a pool.
5. Making raised beds—an alternative.
6. Producing the planting plan.
7. Planting.

Preparing the ground

First the whole of the marked out base area which the alpine garden will occupy should be dug over. On the assumption that large areas will be built up above the existing ground level it will be sufficient if these are cultivated to one full spades' depth but areas not to be built up should be cultivated to two full spades' depth. The second spit, at whichever level it occurs, will be the subsoil of the alpine garden and this should be improved along the same lines as the future topsoil into which the alpines will be planted, but on a more modest scale. This will involve, for the average garden soil, the addition of peat, leaf-mould or well made compost and also plenty of gritty material to help the drainage, such as sharp sand, grit, chippings or mortar rubble. The quantities to be used must depend on the nature of the soil, but the subsoil must be made to drain readily and yet be a good medium to attract the plant roots reaching into it in search of moisture and nourishment. To this end a good sprinkling of bone meal should also be incorporated.

The elevated areas will, in most cases, require some extra bulk. If it has been decided to include a pool as part of the design, the soil from its excavation will go a long way towards providing the bulk for this mounding up. Another source of extra soil will be from the paths, if these are included in the design, as they can be exca-

6

vated and filled in with stones, flints or any other such waste materials. This replacement will be an advantage in a second way as it will further assist the drainage. If still further soil is needed it will have to be secured from another part of the garden, unless a load or two can be obtained from some outside source. There is, however, often a corner of the garden where a large hole can be dug, to be filled in later with garden waste and other rubbish.

Sufficient soil having now been gathered together for the mounds and other planting areas it will be necessary, as in the case of the subsoil, to mix in additional humus forming material such as peat, leaf-mould or compost and gritty material such as sharp sand, grit or boiler ash. The proportions recommended are two to three parts of good garden soil to one part of humus addition and one part of a gritty addition. With good retentive loam two parts will be sufficient but with less ideal garden soil three parts will be better. A liberal sprinkling of a long lasting fertilizer, such as bone meal or hoof and horn, should be thoroughly mixed in. It must be borne in mind that the alpine garden will go for five, ten or fifteen years without any disturbance or improvement other than top-dressing from time to time. Even aristocratic alpine plants have to feed and it is most discouraging to see them running out of steam and deteriorating after a few years. In one's first alpine garden it is as well to provide a good growing medium suitable for a wide range of easier yet very rewarding alpine plants and then, later on, with increasing experience the building of screes, peat beds, etc., for plants with specialised requirements can be tackled.

All that has been written so far has assumed that the novice's garden is not on an acid soil and that he will not initially be growing such acid-loving plants as dwarf rhododendrons, summer flowering heathers and so on. Whether the soil is acid can be ascertained by the use of one of the simple testing kits that can now be bought quite inexpensively. Alternatively a neighbouring gardener may be able to put him wise or he may be able to deduce the fact from observing whether rhododendrons and heathers thrive readily in the neighbourhood. In old gardens, however, beware of lime added in the past which may still be present in sufficient quantities to cause yellowing or even death of calcifuge plants. As it happens that the larger number of alpine species grow in nature on limestone formations, it is recommended that the novice defers attempting to grow plants demanding acid conditions until a further stage in his alpine progress—that is unless he is gardening on a naturally acid soil. Should the latter be the case then for the majority of plants, which prefer alkaline or neutral conditions, he may need to neutralise the acidity with heavy dressings of chalk or lime. It will be even better if he can import a lorryload of good fertile non-acid soil to be used in making up his mixture since many acid soils are also not very good growing media in other respects for the majority of plants.

7

Naturally, for the acid loving plants he can retain a portion of the alpine garden in its acid condition.

In one successful alpine garden that the writer made, he used large quantities of weathered boiler ash from his coal-fired household boiler and this proved a priceless addition to his very chalky soil, providing a long lasting supply of many minerals including trace elements. Also the grittiness of the soil encouraged extremely good root systems on most plants. Nowadays coal-fired boilers are becoming rather scarce but sometimes waste heaps of gritty ash are encountered. Mention is made of this source to emphasise the need to look around either in the garden or in one's neighbourhood to see what potentially useful materials are available free for the taking, or for a minimal charge. For instance, broken up concrete, old broken bricks and broken tiles are all materials that can be used to advantage in the alpine garden—not, of course, visible on the surface but incorporated lower down where the roots of the alpines will be most appreciative when they strike them. These materials are great moisture retainers and yet helpful also to the drainage, especially if well broken up. The average alpine gardener is not possessed of a long purse and with the exercise of a little ingenuity he can make a very good alpine garden without bankrupting the family! If a building is being demolished in the neighbourhood a little friendly liaison with the builder or contractor will often secure useful material at small cost, even perhaps including good stone from an overgrown Victorian garden in extreme cases of good luck! Another source of valuable material is odd corners of local builders' yards where there are often caches of old recovered stone and other materials which have been forgotten about for many years and which they are often glad to be rid of for a small sum. The exercise of a little ingenuity in the procurement of one's materials is definitely to be recommended.

Selecting the stone

Before any contouring or construction can start it is necessary for the stone to have been selected and brought on site. Which kind of stone should be chosen? The answer for the beginner will usually be that which can be got hold of at a reasonable cost, for transport of such a heavy material is very expensive if it has to be brought far. If he is in a district where stone outcrops or is quarried then normally that is the stone to go for. It may not be the perfect stone in either appearance or properties but with weathering, either natural or speeded up, its appearance can be improved greatly and, once partially covered by the planting, it will probably soon fit harmoniously into the scene. Blocks of chalk should never be used, nor are large flints suitable.

Naturally occurring stone or rock falls broadly into three categories:

    (a) Granites
    (b) Limestones
    (c) Sandstones.

The least desirable are granites as they are so hard that weathering agents make very little impact on them. Also, not being porous, they are not very friendly to plant growth. However, even these hard rocks can be used if there is no alternative, though the planting will have to be carefully arranged to soften their usually austere and angular outlines. Many different alpine plants grow in the wild on granitic formations but not so many as those which grow on the limestone formations.

The stone to which most people will have access, if any, will in all probability be either a sandstone or a limestone. The limestones probably have the edge as a class in providing the most attractive and useful rocks, starting with Westmorland (prohibitively expensive but very beautiful) and proceeding through the limestones of Yorkshire, Derbyshire, Purbeck, and Cheddar, all of which are very good for alpine garden purposes. Magnesium limestone from the Cotswolds is also good, though light in colour, whilst the oolite of the same area tends to crumble rather too easily in frosty conditions. Some very useful sandstones occur in Surrey and Sussex as well as in Cheshire, Worcester and the Forest of Dean. Kentish ragstone is another stone which is sometimes offered—it is very hard and weathers only slowly but is, nevertheless, acceptable where available locally.

If no local stone is available there is no need to despair as artistic and satisfying alpine gardens have, in the face of necessity, been made with large lumps of broken concrete! That of the late Reginald Malby, a great alpine expert, was a case in point. Concrete is not to be recommended if natural stone is obtainable, for it involves more skill to make an alpine garden look well using a material with no natural stratification or bedding planes. There are similarities between lumps of broken concrete and the conglomerate rock sometimes encountered in the mountains. The latter is a rock formed under great heat from pebbles, etc., set in a matrix of molten material which has set. Where broken concrete is used, only the broken faces should be visible and these, painted with a solution of iron sulphate, will soon darken and appear more natural. The arrangement of the planting over the concrete can do much to screen its artificial nature. The separate pieces of concrete should be so arranged in relation to each other as to suggest approximate stratification and not be disposed in a random manner, or the effect will be a very sorry one.

Another possibility in the absence of a supply of natural stone is to make one's own rocks from a mixture of two-and-a-half parts sand, one part cement and one-and-a-half parts horticultural peat. It will be necessary to make a mould in a bed of sand or loose soil of the shape required and then pour the mixture in. The rock, if taken out after twenty-four hours, will still be sufficiently soft to be scored or otherwise treated with a hammer and cold chisel to make it look more natural and weathered. If well made, such rocks can appear very close to the real thing. Artificial rocks can nowadays be bought at garden centres but they are fairly expensive and do not usually look very convincing.

Contouring the ground and fixing the rocks

With the soil prepared and the rocks to hand the exciting moment has arrived when the creative side of the work begins. There is no doubt that the creative outlet that the making of an alpine garden gives is one of the reasons why, against all odds, the building of such gardens is likely to continue, even if in a somewhat modified form. Such gardens are particularly pleasing to those who have enjoyed the beauty of these little plants in their natural settings. Even in the mountains they can be seen growing in the short mountain turf in relatively flat areas with only an occasional rocky outcrop. If the supply of rocks is limited then this type of setting should be our model, rather than that of masses of rocks and vertical rock faces.

There are countless ways in which an alpine garden can be arranged, and therein lies the fascination. The success of the completed work must always be a measure of the taste and powers of observation of the builder, who must be prepared to do and to undo each successive stage many times until he is finally satisfied with the result. There is a rightness about the ideal arrangement of each section which, with perseverance, must finally emerge. No individual rock must look wrong in relation to its fellows and yet the arrangement must not look forced and artificial, with the hand of man only too clearly declaring itself.

In Figure 1 I have illustrated one possible arrangement using a minimum amount of rocks. It shows in plan form a small alpine garden made on a flat area together with, in elevation, a cross section along the line ABCD. It will be noted that the arrangement and tilt of the rocks is consistent with the way they might occur in nature. The parallel lines of stratification have been marked in lightly showing the strata dipping back into the soil or, if one prefers to regard it another way, outcropping from the soil at a regular angle of about ten degrees. Here the rocks only outcrop in three places and these outcrops occupy only a little over a quarter of the surface of the alpine garden, the remainder consisting of the gentle reverse slopes. The planting on these slopes should simulate that occurring naturally over the top strata of an outcrop, usually a short alpine turf thickly set with low carpeting alpines. In the garden it will probably be necessary to leave out the grass element and concentrate on the mat-forming alpines such as mossy saxifrages, gypsophila, creeping phlox and other choice alpines of the same habit. To avoid excessive drying out an area raised about $1\frac{1}{2}$ ft. at its highest point should preferably be not less than about $7\frac{1}{2}$ ft. in width.

To achieve this effect of stratified outcropping it is obviously an advantage to have rocks that display some signs of their original bedding planes, i.e. a long axis where each split off from the underlying bedrock and a short axis representing the thickness of the slice of detached rock. Where these indications exist they must be

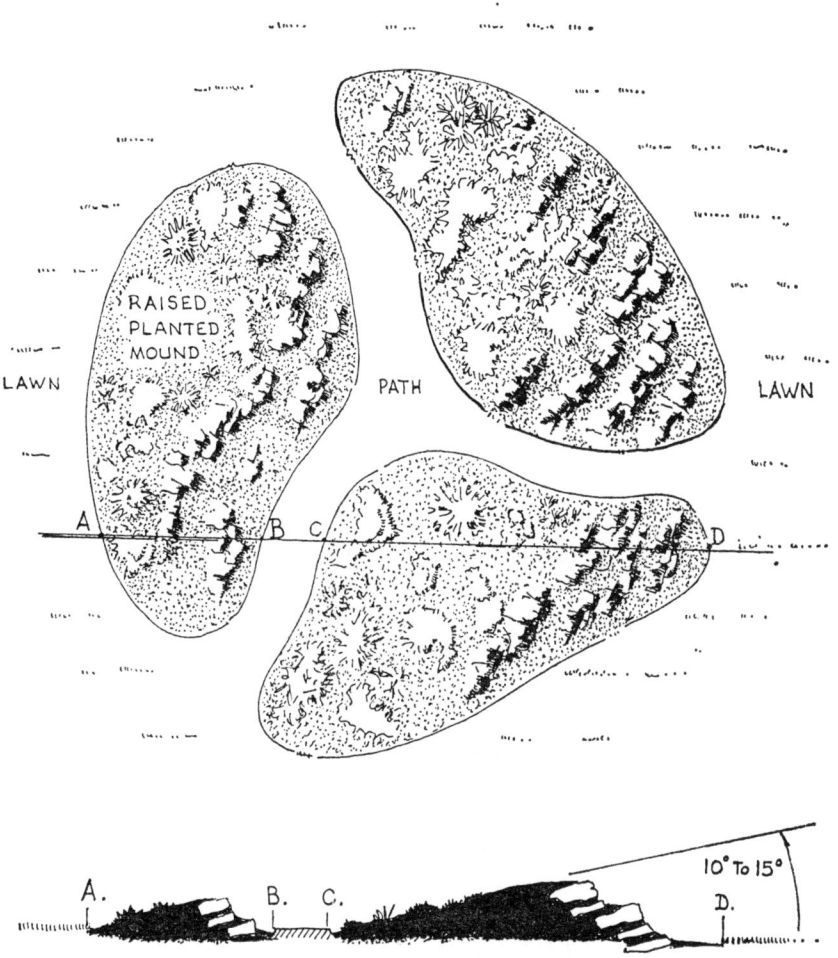

ELEVATION ALONG LINE A.B.C.D.

Figure 1

respected in the way that the rocks are laid. Some rocks, however, show no such visible indications and may be of a lumpy configuration. Figure 2 shows stratified rocks, the parallel lines indicating the planes of stratification, bedded firmly into the soil of the steeper slope, from which they are outcropping, so as to give an overall natural effect and to provide convenient niches for the growing of the choicer alpines. Rocks showing no stratification or pieces of weathered concrete can also be arranged to give this effect but obtaining a convincing result will make considerably greater demands on the builder's skill.

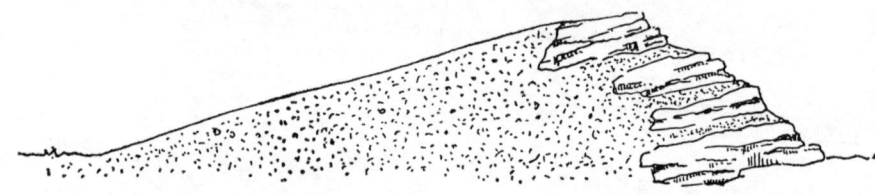

Figure 2

It may be objected that in such a design much of the elevated area is not held up by rocks and that the rain will wash the soil downhill instead of being caught and directed towards the roots of the plants. This is, however, to overlook the fact that one of the most essential parts of modern alpine gardening is the top-dressing of the whole of the surface with a covering of one or two inches of stones or chippings. Their presence serves several very useful purposes. Firstly they minimise soil erosion, secondly they help to keep the ground cool and moist, thirdly they help to keep down weeds and fourthly, where weeds grow, they make their removal much easier. Even though in the initial stages a torrential downpour may displace some of the chippings, once the growth of the mat-forming plants has got under way very little trouble should be experienced on this score and the plants will definitely appreciate this stone mulch and grow more healthily for its presence. Even in alpine regions the ground is usually covered with plant growth except in the places where the surface is bare rock. Thus our aim should be not to produce pockets of soil containing one or two lonely looking specimens surrounded by soil but rather to produce a more or less complete ground cover of planting.

If the supply of rocks is on a more generous scale a more traditional form of construction such as is shown in Figure 3 may be preferred. Here again the construction is shown in plan form and also in elevation along a cross-section ABCDEFG (Figure 4). The construction provides pockets and shelves of soil held up by rocks with the occasional built up face of rock in which crevice plants can be placed. It is clear though that this type of layout demands

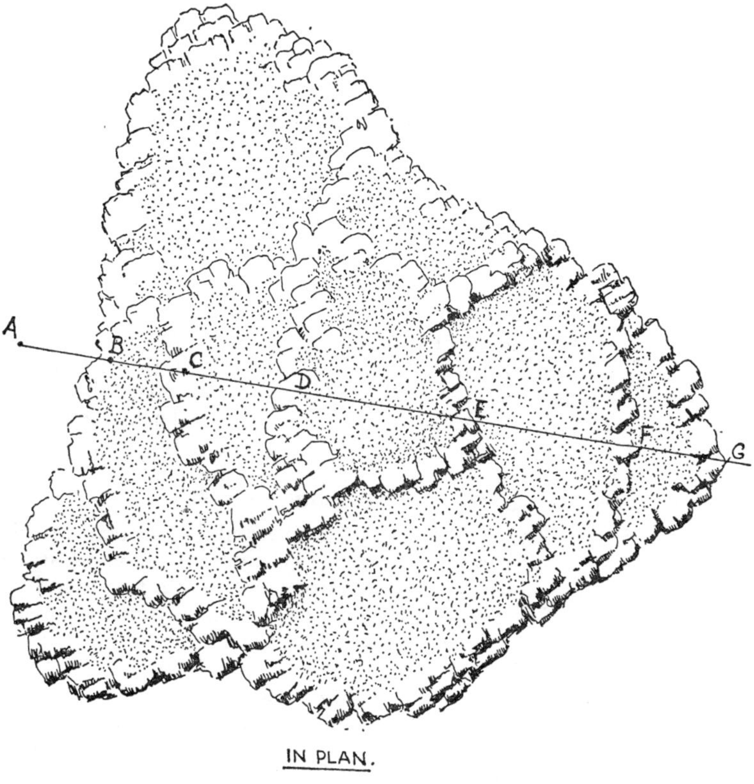

IN PLAN.

Figure 3

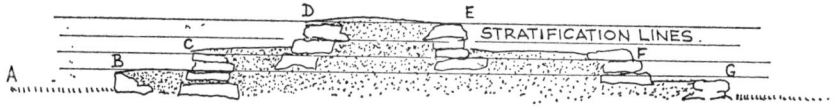

ELEVATION ALONG LINE A.B.C.D.E.F.G.

Figure 4

plenty of stone including rocks of some size if the faces are to be constructed firmly and without risk of subsequent displacement. Particular care must be taken to ensure the stability of any rocks on which the owner or any of his visitors may step to tend or inspect parts of the garden not easily accessible from the paths. For the setting of large or important rocks it is essential that the prepared ground underneath should have had a chance to settle and that the rock should be set firmly so that it is impossible to make it move. This will usually mean that up to half its bulk will be below ground. If it is also having to act in a retaining capacity, the earth added behind it at the higher level must be rammed firmly so that no cavities are left. Normally no cementing is used, so that complete rigidity can only come from painstaking construction, selecting each rock carefully for the role it has to play and then bedding it into position with the utmost care.

In the elevation shown in Figure 4 it will be seen that the stratification lines have been lightly drawn in and that they are all running parallel with the ground. This type of alpine garden can be conceived of as an elevated rocky area from which the previously surrounding material has been weathered away over the years leaving it standing up in isolation. It is a most useful arrangement in furnishing a number of different aspects and situations to suit plants with different requirements and, once the plants get going and tumbling over the rocks, it can look very well.

Figure 5 shows a general plan of a larger alpine garden, in this case incorporating a pool and series of internal stepping stone paths. If alpine flowers and rocks complement each other, then it is the reflecting surface of even a small area of water which seems to complete the picture. The stepping stone paths shown give easy access to all parts of the garden, as well as to all sides of the pool. Nowadays when the provision of pool liners has made pool construction so easy the beginner need not feel any qualms about embarking on such a venture. A pool will be helpful not only scenically in providing a focal point for the alpine garden but also practically, as its excavation will provide a useful supply of topsoil to help build up the elevated areas.

If the garden is being made on level ground then, as already explained, some extra soil will have to be found from elsewhere but if it is made on sloping ground it will be possible to avoid this by cutting into and building out from the slope. On level ground the pool should be at the lowest point of the finished construction to drain the whole. It is important, however, not to omit the provision of an overflow which will involve a length of pipe or hose to take surplus water to a natural outfall, a soakaway or the piped rainwater drainage system. On sloping ground the pool, though not necessarily at the lowest point, can still be made to appear a natural feature if its surroundings are arranged skilfully (see p. 22). In such a case the overflow can, if desired, be into a boggy area lined with simple polythene where moisture-loving primulas and similar plants can be grown. The logical solution would, of course, be a streamlet flowing into the pool from a higher level and trickling out at a lower level. This would, however, normally involve a pump to

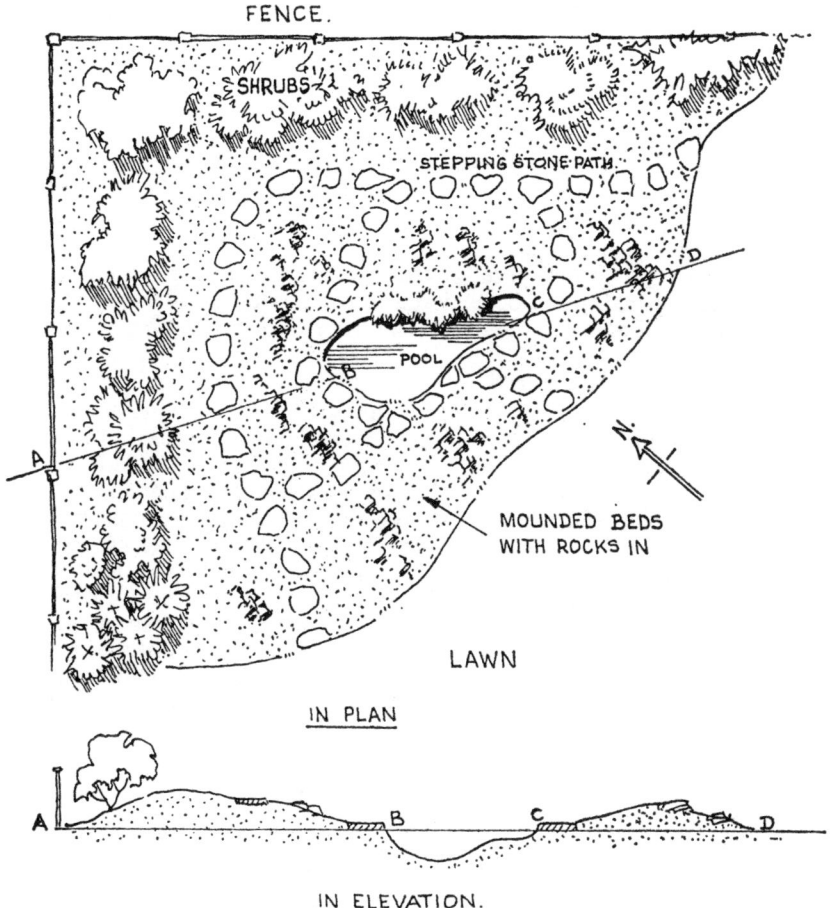

Figure 5

return the water to the higher level if the feature was to be kept running throughout the year and pumps, fountains, streams and other more ambitious uses of water must unfortunately be omitted from the scope of this beginner's guide.

If, as in this case, internal paths are required, the most natural way of providing them is by the laying of flat, irregularly shaped stepping stones of a material which will harmonise with the rocks employed in the alpine garden. They should be laid to suit a short step, with the spaces between them occupied by completely prostrate plants such as Thyme. If this approach is not favoured, or if suitable stepping stones are not available, the paths can be made of gravel or stone chippings. These may seem a little obtrusive at first but they will soon tone down and provide homes for various alpine seedlings (and weeds!) to germinate. With correct treatment the final effect can become very harmonious. The paths to avoid are ones of formal paving and grass, the latter because their narrowness will inevitably mean that they will be unable to take the wear. If, unavoidably, a formal path, paved or otherwise, fronts the alpine garden, informality can be achieved to some extent by allowing the plants to spill out over the path in an irregular manner.

Making and stocking a pool

For beginners the use of a plastic liner is the simplest method of pool construction. These liners vary in durability and price but it is recommended that one should be chosen from about the middle of the price range. As received the liner is simply a rectangular sheet of the chosen material, usually blue on one side and stone-coloured on the other, either of which can be chosen to be the visible surface. For the alpine garden the stone-coloured side looks best. Rigid or semi-rigid pre-shaped pool liners can also be bought but are considerably more expensive and require more careful preparation and shaping of the excavation to receive them. All necessary instructions are received with the liner. It is, however, particularly important that the proposed excavation should be lined with soft sand and/or many thicknesses of newspaper to prevent any stones present in the soil being able to penetrate the liner and cause a leak.

The pool should be about 18 in. deep in the centre to allow a sufficient depth of unfrozen water in the winter for the survival of the fish. The excavation should be shaped to provide a shallower ledge around part of the perimeter for those water plants which can only grow in shallow water (Figure 6). For advice on the choice of this specialised range of plants it is best to rely on the centre where one buys the whole of one's water garden requisites. It is essential for water oxygenating plants to be included as well as ornamentals. The centre should also be asked to supply a variety of water lily appropriate to the size and depth of the pool in order that it does not rapidly take over entirely.

16

A rock garden on the grand scale (see p. 1)   *Photo: Harry Smith Collection*

Campanula portenschlagiana (p. 38)   *Photo: D. F. Merrett*

A simple rock garden using a modest amount of stone (see p. 1)

Photo: R. C. Elliott

Hebe pinguifolia var. *pagei* (p. 39)
Photo: R. C. Elliott

Overleaf: A mature rock garden
Photo: H. L. Crook

A pool adds interest at all times of the year (see p. 16) *Photo: by courtesy of R. B. G. Edinburgh*

Phlox subulata (p. 40)　　　　　　　　　　　Photo: R. C. Elliott

A raised bed—an alternative form of gardening with alpines (opposite)
Photo: D. F. Merrett

The secret of the pool remaining a pleasant ornamental feature rather than an unsightly scum-covered breeding ground for mosquitoes lies in maintaining a balanced population of animal and plant life, in particular of oxygenating plants, fish and molluscs (snails and fresh-water mussels). As these increase and settle in, a further flora and fauna of small water inhabiting insects and micro-organisms will develop. Mosquito larvae will be consumed as part of the fishes' diet.

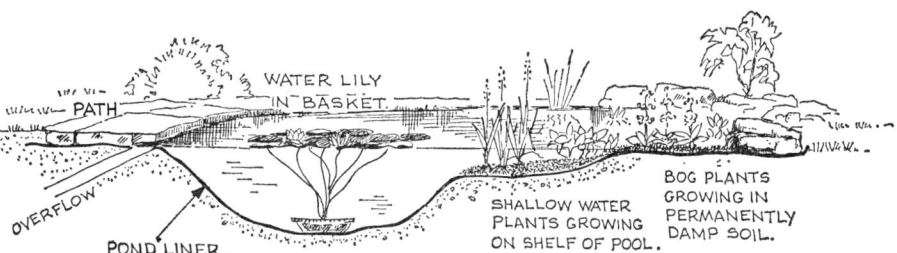

Figure 6

To start with, before a perfect balance has developed, a certain amount of algal scum will rise to the surface, particularly in the spring, and this will have to be skimmed off. As the balance develops this trouble will diminish and finally disappear. As with the plants it is advisable to go to a specialist water garden centre for one's requirements of fish and molluscs. There is no need to keep solely to goldfish—a few golden orfe and golden rudd should also be bought with perhaps a tench as a bottom feeder and scavenger. The number of fish bought must not be greater than is recommended for the size of one's pool.

Making raised beds—an alternative

It is important to realise that, as an alternative to the type of landscaped alpine garden so far described, alpines can also be grown in raised beds held up by dry stone walls, wooden railway sleepers, bricks or even concrete blocks. Such raised beds, if decided upon, should preferably be made no more than 20 in. in height to avoid problems arising from excessive settlement and over-rapid drying out in summer. In point of fact 12 in. is sufficient where the natural drainage of the base soil is good (see p. 24). This method of culture is becoming increasingly popular with keen growers of alpines who are less concerned with the landscaping aspects of their hobby. The result is something that closely resembles trough culture, though on a much larger scale.

Whether stone or some other material is used to retain the soil, the retaining walls must be firmly constructed. Unless bricks or concrete blocks are used little or no cementing will be required, as the soil between the stones will be useful to grow plants in to soften the whole effect. Rather, however, than risk stones falling out at some future date, it may be better to do a little concealed cementing anywhere where it seems to be especially required. Wooden railway sleepers, if obtainable, can be particularly useful for holding up the beds—they should be used one sleeper deep (10 in.) or two sleepers deep (20 in.) according to the efficiency of the drainage of the base soil and according to one's own personal taste and requirements. The sleepers should be laid precisely in line and held in place with iron pickets firmly driven in. If a stone or brick boundary or internal dividing wall already exists it can retain the back of the bed to great advantage, but then the bed must not be more than 4 ft. wide as access to it will have to be from the one side.

The retaining walls having been built, the next requirement is the soil infill, which should be of a prepared mixture made up of two parts garden soil, if fertile and suitable, one part horticultural peat or leaf soil and one part of grit, sharp sand or chippings. If the quality of the soil is in doubt the proportion of soil should be raised to three parts. Such a mixture will drain freely, retain adequate moisture for the plant roots and have sufficient growth potential. A liberal sprinkling of bone meal or hoof and horn should be added when the ingredients are mixed together. With raised beds, as with troughs, the excellent results obtained stem from the good drainage and the properly prepared soil mixture.

After the raised beds have been planted the whole should be covered with a mulch of grit or chippings to a depth of at least an inch and this dressing should be reinforced annually. For variety, interestingly shaped rocks can be partially sunk at intervals over the surface of the bed. If there are soil-filled interstices in the retaining wall these should be planted up with young plants which, as they grow, will much improve the general appearance. If bricks or concrete blocks are used, openings should be left uncemented at intervals to allow for some planting as well as to act as weep-holes.

As the beginner becomes more ambitious in the plants he tries to grow, those which benefit from some overhead protection from damp in the winter can be grouped in one part of the bed so that a suitable overhead covering can be put into position to protect that part.

There is no doubt that the use of raised beds has proved an eminently successful way of growing alpines and this method is recommended as worthy of consideration by all beginners setting out on their alpine Odyssey. Other advantages of raised beds are that they bring the plants up to a level where they can be appreciated at closer quarters and also, at the higher level, it is somewhat easier and pleasanter to work amongst them. They may, however, need a little more attention in the way of watering during dry periods.

Producing the planting plan

The initially produced plan of the alpine garden may or may not have had planting included on it, but in any case when the construction has been completed it is much easier to envisage the desired effects and to work out the planting accordingly. Some authors recommend planting as one proceeds with construction, and there may be certain places where this has to be done, but in general plants suffer if they are repeatedly handled and moved about as construction proceeds, so that nowadays planting is usually treated as a separate operation carried out after construction and before the final top-dressing with stones or chippings.

In advocating the drawing out of a scale planting plan it may be thought that I am obsessed by the drawing of plans. Obviously planting can be done without working from such a plan but the merit of its production is that it makes one think carefully and face up to all the considerations involved. In this way one is far more likely to get a really satisfactory result and to avoid subsequent chopping and changing when errors of spacing and arrangement become apparent. It will also be possible to work out colour schemes, flowering effects throughout the year, the best positions and aspects for different plants and the impact of foliage colours and contrasts. The last point is a particularly important one, which is often overlooked, since the foliage and the general effect of the plants is seen for a much longer period than the floral display.

The plan should also give full weight to the appearance of the alpine garden during the winter months from, say, mid-October to mid-March. Its composition should have sufficient interest, even though on a diminished scale, for one to wish to take a stroll in it during every month of the year. While good foliage effects will make this more rewarding, there are also an appreciable number of plants which produce their flowers during these winter months. To quote a few: winter flowering heathers, *Daphne mezereum*, christmas roses and many late or early flowering bulbs such as cyclamen, winter iris, snowdrops, crocuses and winter aconites. If some of the winter flowering plants can also be positioned where they can be seen from the windows of the house one will secure an additional pleasure.

Dwarf shrubs and dwarf conifers can also contribute to the year round effect, though they must be used with care as in many cases their dwarf character is apt to prove deceptive after a relatively short number of years and removal at that stage both demands resolution and also causes a considerable upheaval. Often they are left *in situ* when they have clearly outgrown their original role, giving an overgrown effect to the alpine garden and changing its character.

The drawing out of the planting plan can give an immense amount of pleasure and from it can be compiled a list of the selected plants together with the quantities required of each. This list can then be marked up with three different symbols to indicate the probable source of supply of the plants.

(a) Plants to be ordered from or chosen at a commercial nursery.

(b) Plants which will hopefully be obtainable from friends' gardens.

(c) Plants which it is proposed to raise oneself either from seed or cuttings.

A definite detailed plan showing how the alpine garden will eventually be planted will provide something to work towards, even if all the plants are not immediately available. For instance, it may have been decided to try and raise some of the plants oneself, perhaps from seed selected from the Alpine Garden Society's annual Seed List. In parenthesis it may be mentioned that one gets far more satisfaction if not all the plants are bought in straight from a nursery and if one has raised some of them oneself. In such a case the spaces intended for these plants will have to be occupied temporarily by "fillers", such as some of the neater growing annuals, which will produce an immediate and often far from unpleasing effect. Annuals are probably the best "fillers" since there is no temptation to leave them in after they have served their purpose.

If one's plan embraces both common and less common plants it will mean that a number will probably be procurable from one's friends, leaving one's expenditure for the less common and more difficult to propagate plants which will inevitably have to be obtained from an alpine nursery.

Planting

If the construction of the alpine garden has been completed in the autumn and early winter then by the spring the winter rains will have caused any settlement to have taken place and planting can be done with confidence, knowing that the plants will not be damaged by winter weather and that the arrival of spring will rapidly enable them to make new growth and settle happily into their new quarters. By the time they have to face the subsequent winter they will be established plants. That does not, however, mean that planting cannot be done if need be at other times of the year as most alpines supplied from nurseries are pot-grown and transplant relatively easily. For plants or bulbs that make their effect in early spring, September–October will be the best time for planting.

When planting it is a good idea to have at hand a barrow load of newly prepared mixture, as already detailed. This having been made up in the dry will be in a nice friable condition to put around the roots and will enable them to be firmed in nicely. If the root balls of pot-grown plants are very compressed, or if the plants seem at all pot-bound, it is a good thing to loosen the root ball and tease out the roots a little to encourage them to grow into the surrounding soil.

The holes for planting should be taken out with a trowel to a sufficient depth to allow roots to be extended to their full length and not to be doubled back on themselves. The roots will also appreciate, where feasible, being placed close to the buried portion of a rock as moisture is always retained there. If planting has to be done in crevices between rocks it will always be more satisfactory to use very young plants or even seedlings as their young roots will soon grow into the recesses of these confined quarters.

SUBSEQUENT CARE OF THE ALPINE GARDEN

Since the initial construction of an alpine garden involves a considerable amount of hard work it is excusable for the beginner to think that on its completion he can legitimately sit back and enjoy the fruits of his labours. To some extent this is true for much of the subsequent success will stem from the conscientiousness with which the initial work has been undertaken. However, as with all forms of gardening, subsequent care has its own special part to play and mention will now be made of the principal operations to which attention will have to be given.

Mulching

Mention has already been made of the importance of surfacing the whole of the alpine garden with stone chippings, grit, pea gravel or whatever similar material can be readily obtained. This stony mulch serves several distinct practical purposes already enumerated to which may be added the gain that the top-dressing, provided it is done with a sympathetic looking material, makes the alpine garden look more natural, as a bare soil surface is rarely if ever seen in the mountains. By one means or another this surface mulch seems over the years to get mixed in with the underlying soil so that it is important each winter for some addition of the same material to be made.

Weeding

The assistance that a stony mulch can give to the work of weeding has already been mentioned. Weeding is particularly important amongst alpines and it has normally to be hand weeding. It is true that various herbicides can be used with care in between most of the plants, and large establishments are increasingly resorting to such aids. However, for the beginner the areas involved are not large and, dare it be said, there is even some satisfaction to be gained from weeding amongst one's small treasures. One gets to know one's plants more intimately and to recognise the self-sown seedlings that are such pleasant discoveries in this area where the dutch hoe does not exact its indiscriminate retribution. These self-sown seedlings can be allowed to grow on *in situ* if suitably placed but more probably they will be useful for subsequent lifting and potting up for one's friends.

Alpine gardens are said to be very labour intensive, involving a large amount of hand weeding. This is debatable—it may or may not be the case according to various circumstances. The most important point is to make a clean start by eliminating *all* perennial weeds before the alpine garden is constructed. If this has been done the problem becomes one of dealing with annual and biennial weeds, which can be a thankless task if they are once allowed to seed freely. One may of course be faced with a perpetual invasion of wind blown seeds from neglected neighbouring land, which is very disheartening. However, the problem usually arises from an indigenous population of weeds having established itself on or adjacent to the alpine garden which, in its early stages, offers a tempting home for weeds endowed with a pioneering spirit. It is at this stage that the battle is often lost or won. In the first year or two a continuing blitz should be waged to remove every single weed before it manages to reach the seeding stage. With the type of weed liable to be troublesome in the alpine garden the period taken to reach the seeding stage can be very brief indeed, only a month to six weeks in the case of the worst offenders and they will even go on growing during the winter.

The worst weed to guard against is usually the Hairy Bitter-cress, a tiny little plant of the Cruciferae that grows only a few inches in height and bears diminutive racemes of white flowers rapidly turning into small elongated seed-pods. It is a regrettable fact that this little plant often arrives with plants from nurseries or other gardens where it has long since gained the upper hand. Therefore a look-out should be kept for it in all plants bought in, particularly in the larger containers in which shrubs are often supplied. If once found growing in the alpine garden it should be searched out as unremittingly as an infection of cholera! Not one single plant should be allowed to reach the seeding stage or the fight may already be going your enemy's way.

Another small annual which one should have in dread is a diminutive oxalis with little clover-like leaves, often tinged purple— *Oxalis corniculata*. Regrettably this is also widespread in some nurseries. It is most troublesome on the lighter soils in the warmer southern counties where it seeds prolifically. On no account must it be allowed to get a toe hold in the alpine garden. Another slightly larger oxalis (*O. corymbosa*) has come in from abroad and has in places become a terrible nuisance as it spreads at an alarming rate by many little bulbils.

Apart from these particularly vicious little annuals other better known and more wide-spread garden weeds such as Groundsel, Common Chickweed, Mouse-ear Chickweed, Petty Spurge, Persian Speedwell and Small-flowered Willow-herb can rapidly become major menaces in the alpine garden if allowed to do so. These are slightly easier to deal with but must again be caught before seeding. Grasses can also be very troublesome weeds, particularly the Annual Meadow-grass. Where, however, the surface is well dressed with chippings these pull out very neatly and easily, again before they have a chance to shed their seeds.

After about two seasons' blitz the crops of weeds should start to fall off and although weeding will never cease to be one of the main routine jobs it should become less onerous. A careful look out must be kept for the odd weed reaching adult size camouflaged in amongst the plants. It is when this stage is reached that the task of hand weeding assumes a more pleasurable aspect for one is in close touch with one's plants and in a good position to observe whether all is well with them or whether enemies such as greenfly or slugs are lurking in the wings.

Care of individual plants

Although in mass the alpine plants in the mountains may look marvellous, individual plants may be far from good specimens. In nature some will be young and healthy looking whilst others will look old and decrepit—individual plants may live no longer than four or five years before they deteriorate and other specimens take over. In any case those kinds which the conditions suit will flourish at the expense of those which are less well suited. In all senses the weak will go to the wall. In the alpine garden we are endeavouring to preserve an artificial balance, with many different species of plants growing in very close proximity in a limited area, yet aiming that every individual plant should be a good specimen. Also, as the plants are growing in softer climatic conditions and in a richer soil, their growth can be expected to be less compact.

Some plants can be left to themselves with little attention from year to year but others benefit from regular seasonal attention, either by way of removing their spent flower spikes or by way of cutting back their whole growth to keep them compact and healthy looking as well as to stop them over-running their neighbours. The encrusted saxifrages and London Pride are examples of those requiring little care whilst rock roses and aubrieta typically benefit from hard cutting back once the peak of their flowering season is past. Broadly speaking, any plant that is proving too aggressive in its spread should be cut back hard so that it does not occupy more room than has been allotted to it in one's plan. It is through the owner not being sufficiently ruthless that an alpine garden gets out of hand and the choicer plants are overwhelmed. Plants that show themselves rapid growers can usually put up with a lot of tough treatment and the right time to dole this out is immediately one sees a problem looming up and before it has a chance to become acute. Where spreading mats of plants require to be reduced in size the best time to do it is immediately after flowering and one should certainly not wait for the arrival of winter to cut back all the plants at the same time.

Feeding

Whilst most owners of alpine gardens probably do not do any regular feeding it would be better in most cases if they did. Certainly that expert, E. B. Anderson, always recommended it. His formula was to sprinkle annually over the alpine garden a dusting of bonemeal and sulphate of potash, 14 oz. of the former to 2 oz. of the latter, giving the beds sufficient to make them look as if they had been dusted with flour. This will soon wash in. This practice will hopefully postpone indefinitely the day of re-making and re-soiling. It is a good common sense practice which prevents the plants living solely on capital. The need for feeding will vary greatly from soil to soil. A soil containing an element of good loam or clay is in a far better position to recharge itself than a light sandy soil.

Adjustments to planting

Whilst the majority of the planting will remain constant, in most years some few changes will be necessary. Certain planting may fail or deteriorate to the point of near failure. A decision has then to be taken whether to replace with the same subject or to concede defeat and go for an alternative planting. The occurrence of a space may be welcomed as providing a home for some newcomer that one has acquired. Whilst changes of this nature are forced upon one, it is always advisable to review the planting from year to year, particularly at the time when it is at its peak. It is then that mistakes become apparent and some mistakes are always bound to creep in long after the novice stage has been passed. It is wrong to put up with anything which jars. Additions may often take the form of extra bulb planting, particularly the many desirable species of crocuses, irises, dwarf daffodils, and the like. These can be added at any stage of the garden's development, preferably being planted where they will shoot up through the most prostrate of carpeting plants. One can hardly have too many of these choice gems.

Adjustments to construction

These should not often occur but any arrangement that jars or is otherwise unsatisfactory should be changed. It is probably not until after at least the first season's growth, and perhaps more, that one can really see whether or not one's plan has succeeded in every respect. It may then be clear that quite a small structural rearrangement will greatly improve the effect.

In other places rocks may be moving, in which case the original setting and firming were at fault and this must now be put right. In particular all stepping stones or rocks which may from time to time be used for stepping on should be tested for firmness and be rebedded and packed with soil if there is any movement.

Maintenance of the pool

If the pool has been sited well away from trees and hence from leaf-fall, if over-vigorous plants, particularly the stronger growing water lilies have been avoided and if plenty of fish, snails and other scavengers have been provided, one will have gone a long way to reducing the sources of trouble. The main reasons that can make the complete cleaning out of a pool necessary are if the depth of water becomes progressively shallower due to a build up of mud on the bottom and if the growth of the plants, particularly water lilies, becomes too overpowering. Providing one's planting has been correct the need for such a drastic operation as a complete clean out can be deferred almost indefinitely by each autumn removing by hand the masses of sodden leaves which will inevitably blow in from somewhere and sink to the bottom. This is a somewhat messy operation and may involve placing a plank or ladder across the pool to lie on. It is, however, well worth while as an annual routine since a complete emptying out and cleaning of the pool, as well as being a major operation involving the finding of temporary quarters for all the fish and other livestock, completely upsets the delicate biological balance that has been slowly achieved and occurrence of trouble with cloudiness and formation of scum may occur, particularly if refilling has had to be done with tap water. If the main plants have been planted in special baskets it will be possible to lift these baskets and divide and replant the plants without too much difficulty.

PROPAGATION

In a guide intended for beginners there is insufficient space to go into the subject in any great detail. There are, however, very good reasons why even the beginner should try his hand at propagating his plants. These are:

1. It will save him money.
2. Success will give him great satisfaction and boost his confidence.
3. He will gain a better understanding of his plants.
4. He will, if an A.G.S. member, be able to make use of its Seed Distribution Scheme.
5. He will have a supply of young plants to experiment with and to exchange with his friends.

The beginner need only be concerned with three methods of propagation—division, seed and cuttings.

Division

Where applicable this is the simplest method. It is, however, only possible with those plants which form a cluster of crowns at ground level or which make rhizomes or stolons capable of detachment. Plants with tap-roots cannot be divided as each division must have its own separate quota of roots. If in doubt about the applicability of this method a trial can easily be made—it will soon be clear if it is not possible to detach a portion with roots. Freshly made divisions should either be planted out into a prepared nursery bed or, if planted in their final position, the soil should have been improved by the incorporation of peat and sharp sand or similar materials.

The so-called "Irishman's Cutting" is really only a form of division, being a stem which has made a few roots into the soil and which can be detached and treated as a rooted cutting. Many heathers for instance behave in this way. Ideally such a cutting is best potted up and grown on for a season, the same as a normally rooted cutting, but it can be planted out like a division if it seems to have sufficient root and the planting position is similarly prepared.

It is worth mentioning that some plants, including many primulas and the rhizomatous irises, benefit considerably from being divided and replanted in a good soil at regular intervals.

The division of most subjects is best carried out either after flowering or, perhaps more safely for the beginner, in early autumn, say September or early October, when the newly separated pieces can still make new roots without the risk of setbacks from sunny, drying out conditions.

Seed

Propagation from seed is, in most cases, well within the range of the beginner. The main complication with the seed of many alpine plants is that it may be very slow in germinating—in a considerable number of cases this will take over twelve months—the seed having to go through the full cycle of the seasons before its mysterious internal forces can be released by the breaking of dormancy. One must not be discouraged by this, for not all alpines behave in this manner and in fact with such plants as anemones, primulas, cyclamen, pulsatillas and many others, if only seed can be collected from your own or a friend's plants and sown straight away, early germination will take place. This seed, if it had been left to dry off for a month or two, would have lain dormant for at least twelve months.

Even where the long wait is unavoidable it is still worth sowing the tardy germinators and leaving the pots out of doors fully exposed to the elements, but in a shady place where they will not rapidly dry out. One day in the early spring of the subsequent or a later year one will have the thrilling surprise of suddenly discovering the first seedlings making their appearance in pots which had seemed lifeless for so long. With this long dormancy it is most important to see that the surfaces of the pots are dressed with a material which will prevent the growth of moss and which will also stop heavy rain from washing away the seeds. Limestone or granite chippings, chicken grit or the coarse sievings from sharp sand are the best materials for this purpose. If the seed is very fine, which can be the case with a number of alpines, it can be sown on top of the dressing and when the pots are immersed in water it will be sucked down into the interstices of the chippings. If so fine as to be difficult to handle the seed can be mixed with a little silver sand before sowing. Larger seeds can be sown before the dressing is applied.

For seed sowing a mixture of two parts of John Innes Seed Compost and one part of sharp sand is suitable for any but acid-loving plants, for which an acid compost must be substituted. This mixture will drain freely and yet will encourage a good root system in the young seedlings. To prepare the pot a crock or a circle of perforated zinc should be placed over the drainage hole before filling a quarter full with chippings or similar material to ensure rapid drainage, followed by the compost which is gently firmed and levelled before sowing the seeds. Plastic pots are perfectly suitable for seed raising, in fact if many seeds are to be sown, cream or yoghurt pots, which are readily come by, will serve well and not take up too much room. One of these will generally contain sufficient seedlings of any one species for the amateur's needs. In fact unless the seeds have been sown very thinly, or the germination is poor, it will be necessary at a fairly early stage to thin them out with a pair of tweezers. The remainder will need to be pricked out into pots or trays when they have developed three or four small leaves but if they are bulb seedlings they should be left in their seedling pots for the first season. After being pricked out into their new quarters, seedlings must be shaded from direct sun for the first ten days.

Cuttings

Though the raising of certain more difficult plants from cuttings can call for considerable skill and knowledge, there are many which respond to this form of propagation very readily as for instance the rock roses, dwarf violas, creeping phlox and aubrieta. It is not even necessary for the beginner to achieve a 100% strike in his early attempts provided he obtains sufficient young plants for his purposes. In some cases even two or three new young plants may be very welcome.

The first two matters to be considered are the type of shoot from which the cuttings should be made and the time of year such cuttings should be taken. There is in fact a relationship between the two. For the majority of spring flowering alpines the growths which will make good cuttings arise after flowering and are usually in a good condition to be detached in June or early July when they will make what are termed semi-ripened cuttings. Cuttings taken then are best made fairly small, the size ranging with the size of the subject but within the range of 1.5–4 cm. ($\frac{1}{2}$–$1\frac{1}{2}$ in.). They should be cut off just below a node and the lower leaves, which would often be below the surface of the soil, should be carefully trimmed off before the cutting is inserted into the rooting compost to a depth of half its length. If a carton of low strength hormone rooting powder is available the base of the cutting may be dipped in the powder, but this is by no means essential.

With most subjects it is also possible to take cuttings of more fully ripened wood in early autumn, August–September, and these should usually be taken a little larger, 4–7.5 cm. (1½–3 in.), but again the size varies considerably with the size of the subject. These autumn cuttings will probably need to be kept covered until the spring as many will form callus at the base in the autumn, roots emerging from these calluses in the spring.

The polythene bag and pot method, illustrated in Figure 7, is one to be recommended for simplicity and effectiveness. The pot, say a 12.5 cm. (5 in.) clay pot for preference, should be filled with a mixture of 50% peat and 50% sharp sand and then tapped on a surface to settle the contents to 1.75 cm. (½ in.) below the rim. The cuttings should then be inserted at intervals around the perimeter with a few more in the centre. At the same time three thin sticks or hoops of wire, which will support the polythene covering, should be inserted. The pot should then be stood in water to soak for a few minutes before being removed and the polythene bag being put over and fixed in position by an elastic band around the pot. One can if one wishes buy pots with rigid plastic covers but this is not necessary. The polythene bags used must not have any holes in them.

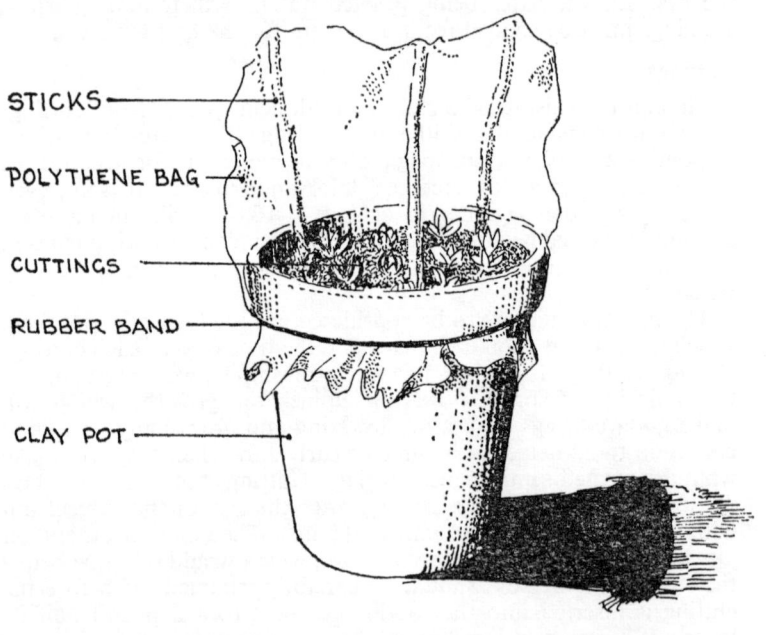

Figure 7

When it can be seen that the cuttings are starting to make growth one of them should be very carefully lifted to check whether rooting has occurred, being carefully re-inserted afterwards. If satisfactory rooting has occurred the polythene bag should be removed. This stage may be reached in about six weeks in the case of cuttings taken in June but not so rapidly in the case of autumn cuttings. The beauty of this method of taking cuttings is that a small batch can be taken at any one time, each pot being confined to the cuttings of one subject, which will all root at about the same time.

Another method of rooting cuttings which may be mentioned, and which is perhaps even more suitable for the cuttings taken in September, is to make a simplified form of frame by taking a wooden box and knocking the bottom out of it, half sinking it in the ground, lightening the soil inside by the addition of peat and sharp sand and inserting the cuttings directly into this in rows. In place of the bottom of the box a sheet of glass should be laid on the sides, held down firmly by weights so that it cannot blow off. Until the cuttings are rooted the box must be shaded. When rooting has taken place the glass should be removed as also can the box if so desired.

Where small cuttings of such plants as kabschia saxifrages or heathers are being taken, they can be inserted in a large round or square pan with a sheet of glass laid over the top. Square pans, 9 in. by 9 in. if available, are very convenient as they will take with ease eight rows of eight cuttings to the row, each row being devoted to a separate variety.

One of the merits of propagating alpines from cuttings is that the newly produced plants will be identical in every way with the individual plant chosen for propagation. In the case of reproduction by seed one is faced with a degree of variability which may be either an advantage or a disadvantage. The other merit of propagation from cuttings is that a better and more shapely plant is normally obtained in this way than by simple division.

FIFTY RECOMMENDED ALPINES FOR THE BEGINNER

There are so many desirable alpines that any selection of fifty plants must be invidious and open to criticism. However, it is thought that it will be helpful to the beginner to have a short list of recommendations from which to make his initial choice. The list contains some low shrubs but dwarf conifers and bulbs are listed separately. All plants are of easy culture. Should the beginner have an acid soil he will also be able to grow the full range of heathers and dwarf rhododendrons but these acid-loving plants are excluded from the present list.

Achillea x argentea 15 cm. Forms tufted mats of attractive finely cut grey foliage bearing white daisy flower heads in compact inflorescences. Long flowering. June–August. Sun.

Aethionema grandiflorum 22 cm. Sub-shrub with attractive grey-blue foliage and spikes of soft pink flowers. Grows freely from self-sown seedlings. May–June. Sun.

Alyssum saxatile 25 cm. Common but indispensable. Grey-leaved slightly untidy plant completely covering itself with rich golden flowers in April–May. Var. *citrinum* pale lemon. Prune back after flowering. Sun.

Androsace sarmentosa 10 cm. Mats of 3 cm. diameter rosettes spreading by runners and bearing numbers of soft pink flowers on 7.5 cm. stems. May–June. Sun.

Antennaria dioica var. **rosea** 5 cm. Dense prostrate mats of silvery leaves bearing modest pink inflorescences. A good carpeter between stones. May–June. Sun.

Arabis 'Rosabella' or **'Rosea'** 10 cm. Probably a hybrid of the common white arabis but prettier and far less rampant. Pink flowered. April–May. Sun.

Aubrieta deltoidea 10 cm. Common but indispensable. An excellent carpeter which shows at its best when hanging down in a curtain of colour. Available in lavender, blue, pink, red and purple shades. Should be cut back hard after flowering. April–May. Sun.

Campanula carpatica 22 cm. A vigorous but very desirable alpine bell flower with large cup-shaped open flowers. The Campanula genus is one of the backbone genera of the alpine garden. Cultivars with white, blue or purple-blue flowers are available but it is typically blue flowered. July–August. Sun.

Campanula cochlearifolia (syn. *C. pusilla*) 7.5 cm. Very dainty and low-growing and spreads extensively by underground shoots, particularly if the soil is rather gritty. The small flowers are blue and bell-shaped but a white form is also available. There is an attractive double, blue-flowered hybrid of this and the foregoing species called *C.* x *haylodgensis*. June–July. Sun.

Campanula garganica 15 cm. Sprays of light blue starry flowers rise from tufts of neat foliage. June–August. Sun.

Campanula portenschlagiana (see p. 17) 10 cm. Common but indispensable. Broad spreading mats of neat foliage bear sheets of purple-blue bell-flowers. It has a very long flowering season; June–September. Sun or half-shade. Not to be confused with *C. poscharskyana* which is extremely invasive.

Daphne mezereum. A rather erect deciduous shrub growing 60 cm. or more in height and flowering before its leaves unfold in February–March. Forms with white, pink, and purple-rose flowers are available, the latter being the typical colour. The flowers almost cover the stems making it very showy so early in the year. It bears red berries. Shade, half-shade or sun.

Dianthus deltoides, The Maiden Pink, 5 cm. Growth pr ostrate with rather dingy green foliage from which pink or bright red flowers on 15 cm. stems arise in profusion. It is worth buying a good cultivar with rich red flowers such as 'Wisley'. Self-seeds readily. July–August. Sun. The pinks are one of the backbone genera of the alpine garden.

Dianthus gratianopolitanus (syn. *D. caesius*), The Cheddar Pink, 15 cm. It bears pale pink fragrant flowers with grey foliage. May–June. Sun.

Dianthus 'La Bourbrille' 5 cm. A choice hybrid forming very decorative prostrate mats of silvery-grey leaves studded in June with small pink flowers on short stems. Sun.

Erica carnea 15–22 cm. Does not need an acid soil as do most other Heathers. The growth is dense but spreading. Valuable for flowering from December to April if several cultivars are planted. 'Springwood White' is white-flowered, mat-forming and roots as it goes. 'King George' and 'Winter Beauty' are rose-crimson flowered and the first to flower. 'Atrorubra' is deep pink and late-flowering. Sun.

Erinus alpinus 10 cm. A closely tufted little plant bearing white, pink or crimson flowers. It is not long-lived but self seeds freely to decorate odd corners of the alpine garden. 'Dr. Hanele', deep crimson, and 'Mrs. Charles Boyle', pink, are good cultivars. May–June. Half-shade or sun.

Genista lydia 40 cm. A low spreading shrub which completely covers itself with bright yellow pea flowers in May and June. It looks well tumbling over a rock but needs 0.75 to 1 m. space. Sun.

Gentiana septemfida 15 cm. Bears bright blue, bell-shaped flowers in clusters at the ends of the stems. July–August. Half-shade or sun.

Geranium dalmaticum 12 cm. Bears cushions of deeply lobed leaves and quantities of beautiful pink flowers in succession from June to August. Sun.

Hebe pinguifolia var. **pagei** (see p. 19) (syn. *H. pageana*) 22 cm. A low spreading evergreen shrub with handsome glaucous grey foliage producing tightly packed spikes of white flowers in April and May. Sun.

Helianthemum nummularium 22–35 cm. The well known "Rock Roses" are very useful in the alpine garden but must be given adequate room and must be cut back each year after flowering. They carry some flower throughout the summer but the main flowering is from May to July. 'Ben Dearg' coppery-pink, 'Ben Fhada', golden-yellow with orange centre, 'Watergate Rose', wine-red, and many other fine cultivars offer a rich choice. Sun.

Hutchinsia alpina 5 cm. Forms low spreading mats of bright green foliage set with inflorescences of little white flowers. Very typical of the Alps. May–June. Sun.

Hypericum olympicum 15–22 cm. A dwarf, bushy St. John's Wort bearing large golden flowers in quantity from June to August. Self seeds freely. Old plants may die out in a hard winter, but young plants will carry on. Sun.

Iberis sempervirens 'Little Gem' 15 cm. The best and most compact shrubby candytuft for the alpine garden, covering itself with white flowers in May. Sun.

Iris pumila 15 cm. Bears almost stemless large purple, blue, yellow or white flowers according to cultivar chosen. A dwarf Flag Iris. April–May. Sun.

Linum 'Gemmell's Hybrid' 22 cm. A sub-shrub with flattish heads of deep yellow flowers. Very showy. May–June. Sun.

Mazus reptans 2.5 cm. A delightful, completely prostrate carpeter bearing small lilac snapdragon flowers which is most useful between stepping stones. May–June. Half-shade or sun.

Papaver alpinum 15–22 cm. Produces very dainty white, orange, yellow or pink poppy flowers. Grows readily from seed. June–July. Sun.

Phlox subulata (see p. 23) 10 cm. A wide-spreading mat requiring trimming back after flowering if neighbouring plants are not to be overwhelmed. It is, however, so floriferous and beautiful that it cannot be omitted from any alpine garden. Recommended cultivars are 'Temiscaming', reddish-purple, 'G. F. Wilson', pale lavender, 'Betty', pink. April–May. Sun.

Polygonum vaccinifolium 15 cm. A prostrate plant which looks particularly well growing over rocks. It has the merit of carrying its erect spikes of soft pink flowers, reminiscent of a heather, in September and October. Does not like very chalky soils. Half-shade or sun.

Potentilla aurea 7.5 cm. Forms prostrate mats of bright green strawberry-like leaves set with rich golden yellow flowers. Also a good double form, Plena. May–July. Sun.

Primula auricula 15 cm. The leaves are covered with white farina and the flowers of the wild species are a rich golden yellow. It grows typically in rocky clefts in the wild. The yellow wild form is recommended for the alpine garden in preference to the more sophisticated florist's forms. April–May. Half-shady fissures, etc.

Primula denticulata. Carries globular heads of lilac coloured flowers on 25 cm. stems. Good white and ruby-red cultivars are also available. Likes a moist rich soil. March–April. Half-shade.

Primula 'Wanda' 7.5 cm. The Common Primrose crossed with *P. juliae* has produced a very good range of colourful hybrids of which 'Wanda', deep red-purple, is the commonest. 'E. R. Janes', salmon-pink, is also good as are several others in different shades of blue and red. Likes a moist soil. March–April. Half-shade.

Pulsatilla vulgaris, The Pasque Flower, 15–20 cm. Bears very lovely lavender-purple flowers amidst finely cut foliage. Cultivars with red, pink, and white flowers are available. Grows well from freshly sown seed but it is best to start with a plant. April. Sun.

Saponaria ocymoides 15 cm. A vigorous trailer which completely covers itself with bright pink flowers. Good on a wall or bank. May–June. Sun.

Saxifraga paniculata (syn. *S. aizoon*) 22–30 cm. The genus Saxifraga is one of the backbone genera of the alpine garden. It is divided into a number of sections, the members of which differ greatly in appearance. *S. paniculata* is the easiest of the Encrusted or Silver section, with small silvery rosettes bearing upright spikes of pale creamy flowers. There is also a good rose-coloured form, 'Rosea'. June. Half-shade or sun.

Saxifraga cochlearis var. **major** 15 cm. Another encrusted species with very ornamental lime-encrusted leaves from which emerge spikes of pure white flowers in May and June. Half-shade or sun.

Saxifraga cotyledon 45 cm. An Encrusted species with large (7.5–10 cm.) ornamental rosettes producing arching sprays of many white flowers spotted lightly with pink. June–July. Half-shade or sun.

Saxifraga x apiculata 7.5 cm. This is the best representative of the Kabschia or Cushion Saixfrages to grow in the open alpine garden. Its profuse primrose-yellow flowers are produced very early in the year in March. A good white cultivar of the same is also obtainable. Half-shade or sun.

Saxifraga 'Sanguinea Superba' 15 cm. This is one of the best hybrids of the Mossy section, forming a close carpet of mossy foliage that is decorative throughout the year. It bears a host of flowers of a rich non-fading crimson. April–May. Half-shade.

S. 'Pixie' is a smaller and neater cultivar with rose-red flowers on 7.5 cm. stems.

Sedum spathulifolium purpureum 7.5 cm. Forms a close prostrate mat of glaucous, purple, fleshy leaves later becoming white and mealy. 'Capa Blanca' is a white cultivar. May–June. Sun.

Sedum spurium 'Schorbusser Blut' 7.5 cm. The foliage is bronze-tinted and the flowers a deep carmine crimson. It will grow in poor soil or a difficult corner. July–August. Half-shade or sun.

Sempervivum arachnoideum 10 cm. The Cobweb Houseleek. The rosettes are small with the incurving leaves cobweb-tipped. Flowers bright rose-red. June–August. Sun.

Sempervivum tectorum 22 cm. The Common Houseleek as seen on roofs. The succulent leaves are green with deep red tips. The flowers are dull purplish-red. There are many superior cultivars with interestingly coloured leaves which are very desirable for the alpine garden. 'Commander Hay', 'Malby's Hybrid' and 'Jubilee' all have brilliant red leaves and are amongst the best. July–August. Sun.

Thymus serpyllum 'Coccineus' 2.5 cm. A creeping, mat-like plant with tiny dark green leaves and strikingly colourful inflorescences of a rich crimson. Good on chalky soils. 'Annie Hall', pink flowered, and 'Albus', white flowered, should also be planted. Particularly useful between stepping stones or for bulbs to grow through. June–August. Sun.

Veronica fruticans (syn. *V. saxatilis*) 10 cm. An excellent procumbent sub-shrubby plant carrying terminal sprays of clear blue flowers with red eyes. July–September. Sun.

Veronica prostrata 'Spode Blue' (syn. *V. rupestris* 'Spode Blue') 10 cm. Forms trailing herbaceous mats of foliage set with spikes of china-blue flowers. June–August. Sun.

Viola cornuta hybrids. These dwarf violas are hybrids of *V. cornuta* with *V. gracilis* and possibly other species. They form broad mats covered with flowers throughout most of the summer. *V. cornuta* 'Minor', blue flowered, *V. cornuta* 'Alba', white flowered, 'Haslemere', lilac-pink flowered, and 'Hunterscombe Purple', deep violet flowered are all strongly recommended. They are invaluable in the alpine garden on account of their long flowering season.

FIFTEEN RECOMMENDED DWARF BULBS OR CORMS FOR THE BEGINNER

The alpine garden is the ideal place to grow dwarf bulbs or corms, apart from those which are woodlanders or are very aggressive in their habits. Amongst the latter are the Grape Hyacinth and the Star of Bethlehem which have been omitted as, although there are choice varieties which are not aggressive, those which the beginner is likely to encounter may well be difficult to eliminate once established. The following fifteen species and their varieties are all of easy culture and can be recommended.

Chionodoxa luciliae 10 cm. Has charming blue flowers with white centres. Increases readily on almost all soils. March–April. Sun.

Crocus flavus (syn. *C. aureus*) 7.5 cm. The Common Yellow Crocus is descended from this species. The species, however, is superior as it naturalises readily and flowers even earlier. The flowers are a deep golden-orange. February–March. Sun.

Crocus chrysanthus 7.5 cm. Several different cultivars of this indispensable species should be planted in every alpine garden. All are very dainty and refined. The following are recommended: 'E. A. Bowles', deep butter-yellow feathered with bronze, 'Cream Beauty', deep cream with golden throat, 'Snow Bunting', white and cream with lilac featherings, 'Zwanenburg Bronze', deep orange suffused mahogany. February–March. Sun.

Crocus speciosus 10 cm. Very useful as it flowers in the autumn. Mauve to purple. Increases readily from seed but this is a fault on the right side. September–October. Sun.

Crocus tomasinianus 'Whitewell Purple' 10 cm. Bluish-purple. This cultivar is superior to the species as the latter may increase too freely and become invasive. It is also a better colour. January–March. Sun.

Cyclamen coum (syn. *C. orbiculatum*) 7.5 cm. The leaves are rounded, without jagged edges, and the flowers are rose, magenta or white in colour but of a more dumpy shape than the other species. Succeeds well out of doors unlike some of the species. January–April. Shade or half-shade.

Cyclamen hederifolium (syn. *C. neapolitanum*) 12.5 cm. The leaves are roughly ivy-shaped with jagged edges and beautiful markings. The flowers appear in autumn, which is a valuable character, and are pale pink to red, though a white variety is also available. The most satisfying of all garden cyclamen. August–November. Shade or half-shade.

Eranthis hyemalis, The Winter Aconite, 7.5 cm. Almost a woodland plant but still worth planting in the alpine garden as its bright yellow flowers make such a useful patch of colour in January. It is neater than the larger *Eranthis* x *tubergeni* which can be grown instead if preferred. January–February. Half-shade or sun.

Galanthus nivalis 'S. Arnott' 15 cm. The choicest form of the Common Snowdrop though unfortunately rather expensive, vigorous and with large, perfect flowers. If an even larger and taller type is desired, *G. elwesii* is excellent. Snowdrops should always be transplanted in the leafy condition and not as dried-off bulbs. February–March. Shade or half-shade.

Iris reticulata 15 cm. Flowers deep blue-mauve and very early. There are several good cultivars, 'Cantab', Cambridge-blue, 'Royal Blue', dark blue and 'Hercules', purplish-red. It should have a sunny, well drained position. February–March. Sun.

Narcissus bulbocodium, The Hoop-Petticoat Daffouil, 10–15 cm. Flowers deep yellow. Thrives best in rich moist soil where it increases freely. There is also a lemon-yellow form, var. *citrinus*. March–April. Half-shade or sun.

Narcissus cyclamineus 15 cm. Flowers rich yellow with perianth segments strikingly reflexed. It needs a moist position to succeed and increase. There are, however, now some very good "cyclamineus hybrids" which are easier to grow but somewhat taller, 22–30 cm. One of the following should be chosen: 'February Gold', 'Peeping Tom' or 'Tête-a-Tête'. February–March. Half-shade or sun.

Puschkinia scilloides 7.5–15 cm. The flowers are rather like those of *Scilla sibirica* but are a very pale blue with a greenish-blue stripe down the centre of each segment. It likes damp conditions. March. Half-shade or sun.

Scilla sibirica 'Spring Beauty', The Siberian Squill, 15 cm. The flowers are a strong Prussian-blue. It seeds and increases readily, sometimes a little too readily but should be planted all the same. February–April. Half-shade or sun.

Tulipa tarda (syn. *T. dasystemon*) 10–15 cm. A really dwarf and easy-to-grow species of tulip. Flowers four or more to a stem. Flowers yellow and white with some red outside. Should be planted in a hot, sunny position. April–May. There are other more brilliant and larger tulip species which can also be planted in the alpine garden if a rather more flamboyant effect is not objected to. These include *T. praestans*, *T. kaufmanniana* and *T. linifolia*, amongst others.

FIVE RECOMMENDED DWARF CONIFERS FOR THE BEGINNER

Views differ on the planting of dwarf conifers in the alpine garden, but on the assumption that the beginner may wish to plant at any rate one of them, a short list is given to ensure that he chooses one that really will be slow growing and remain dwarf. Only too often varieties are chosen which in a few years time present a problem, having become larger than desired and yet being too attractive in themselves to be ruthlessly removed. The following can, however, be recommended as being really slow growing and will take a long time to reach 60 cm. in height. They will not be cheap.

Chamaecyparis obtusa 'Nana Gracilis'. This is a very slow-growing and decorative form bearing attractive whorls of dark green foliage.

Chamaecyparis obtusa 'Tetragona Aurea' its dwarf conical form carries erect branches with foliage of an attractive, glossy golden-yellow colour.

Cryptomeria japonica 'Vilmoriniana'. Makes a compact globular form with deep green "mossy" foliage turning bronze in the autumn.

Juniperus communis 'Compressa'. A very dwarf and compact growing form of the much commoner *Juniperus communis* 'Hibernica' the Irish Juniper. It is, however, desirable to get the 'Compressa' form, as the Irish Juniper will, over the years, attain a height of 2–3 m. It is very narrowly columnar in form with attractive grey-green foliage which is somewhat prickly to the touch.

Picea abies 'Nidiformis'. Its densely crowded branches carrying dark green leaves form a small round flat-topped bush with a slight depression in the centre.